VERITE VIEWS

KRITIKA TAK

Copyright © Kritika Tak
All Rights Reserved.

कर्मण्येवाधिकारस्ते मा फलेषु कदाचन।
मा कर्मफलहेतुर्भूर्मा ते सङ्गोऽस्त्वकर्मणि॥

I want to dedicate this book to the young generation firstly. Secondly,

I want to express my gratitude to parents and teachers who constantly

encourage and support me in every way.

Contents

Preface

Writer intro:

Greetings

Myself Kritika Tak, a learner and a self motivated guide. I am at the age where we as youngsters have to make the choices to build ourselves or break ourselves, where we sacrifice to the circumstances, struggle hard and what not.

And so, I have tried to put all such emotional realities in the form of poetry to which we all can relate ourselves in my book "Vérité Views".

Hope the readers will enjoy the journey.

Acknowledgements

Book intro:

"Vérité Views" is a collection of poems with genre of realism and naturalism. It is like a journey with different terminus like of emotions, awareness, knowledge and enjoyment. This book is dedicated to the young generation with a message, that being emotional is good, but sometimes being rationally emotional is also equally important. Hope the readers will find it relatable.

Prologue

Author : Kritika Tak. Best Wishes for your first book with us.

1. THE CHOICE OF LIFE OVER THE PART OF DEATH

Depression is a common illness worldwide, with an estimated 3.8% of the population affected, including 5.0% among adults and 5.7% among adults older than 60 years. The percentage of adults who experienced any symptoms of depression was highest among those aged 18–29 (21.0%), followed by those aged 45–64 (18.4%) and 65 and over (18.4%), and lastly, by those aged 30–44 (16.8%). Women were more likely than men to experience mild, moderate, or severe symptoms of depression and suicides are most common consequences of depression we see so far. So, I tried to put this mental issue from the perspective of a strong mindset, who tries to control the suicidal thoughts and choose to fight, choose to live…

They say, it kills,

The emptiness that can't be refills.

And some say, it can be cured

A little by medicines, a little by deep word

They advise, the worries you have, just share

Now the question is, what if no one is listening there

Then, to whom I'll say,

That episode rued the day
Who will take my worry?
And serve me cup of glory
Whose footsteps will I follow
When every heart here is shallow
Who'll help me to express my worth
Coz, I can't show, maybe am introvert
I can speak only with my close friends,
But I don't have their trends
Am all alone
Don't know, where my supporters have gone
This hardly hitting my mind,
I don't know how will I find
That happiness, I lost
My worth, I lost
That confidence, I lost
My voice, I lost
And lost my patience,
I lost myself in this unkind world
Even the grievance, which could quench my thirst
Don't know, when I'll get them again
Those happy sites, and that lucky lane
Yes…
Am fighting with my inner soul,
With all the efforts, that I can hold
Still the bloody sense of trust that lives in me
Resist the thought to end life in agony

And this time…

I lost everything, except that hope

Which saved my life, and raised the scope

Scope of healing

Scope of living…

Yes, that faith won "The Choice of Life over the Part of Death"!!!

Kritzy

2. BUT LIFE GOES ON...

The background of this poem is credited to "The Seven Ages" poem by Sir William Shakespeare. I tried to present some creative idea to it, that life is like a cycle, if one's ends, other one's starts, and so it remains there in everything we are surrounded with.

With our birth, the fact too born

That the life goes on…

No matter how blissful or torn,

But it goes on…

Here comes the act of seven ages with a thoughtful view

Where start and the end are same, as hard to chew

At first the infant, mewling in mum's arms,

Dandling on dad's knees, mesmerising with his giggling charms

New to this world, new to the dusk and dawn,

Unknown with the fact that life goes on…

Then comes the perky school going boy, running with a big satchel on his back,

As for those little footsteps, entrance gate to classroom was a racing track

But at the end of the day, that tired noony face,

Whining to his mom, it is hard to chase

Teachers ask to get all work done,

With this problem he was left alone

And the age taught him, above all the miseries one needs to be grown,

As the life always goes on…

And then the woeful lover,

Once promised his mistress to love forever

This, the age of patch-ups and heart breaks, that needs to repair,

By penning down all the sighs on paper

Where he begins to learn, with time it comes all ups and down,

No matter how hard, but in all our life goes on…

And then the soldier full of strange oaths, with beards natured fancy,

Jealous in honour with bucket of militancy

Addressing his troop in powerful tone,

About winning reputation with the life goes on…

And then the justice in fair round belly,

With good capon lined eyes looks severely

Full of wise saws, full of knowledge boon,

Experienced about life, how it goes on…

Then comes the sixth age,

Shifting towards lean and slippery pantaphase

Spectacles resting on his nose,

To get a look of vicinities from close

He became a shadow of his youth,

But has to accept the truth
When even the voice has the childish tone,
He's very well aware with the fact of life goes on…
Now the last of all,
After perfectly playing his every role
Here comes the second childishness,
Mere oblivion, sans teeth, sans eyes and complete dullness
Despite devoid of everything, the truth that still exists is,
Life goes on and on…
Even after his last breath,
In this air, in this nature, on the earth…
Kritzy

3. EMPTY CITY WITH CLEAR SKY

The pandemic has taught us many things so far, may it be to care yourself your families, life can be so unpredictive, even the most powerful economies can depress and most importantly nature is something of very high significance. During lockdown human activities of polluting environment has lowered and this actually gave time for the nature to heal. This was observed statistically as well. This poem is depicting that healing process of nature, here city is being personified. Just enjoy reading it!!

Empty city with clear sky,

No more hide and no more shy

Yeas, real beauty everywhere.

Birds chirping and no noise,

Only melodious deep voice

Filled with every colour, flowers are blossoming,

Yes, my city is recovering

She needs some time,

To overcome that uncountable crime

By recollecting all her strength,

She is adorning her every breath

But,

Those cruel enemies of her mind quest,

How, Who and When don't let her rest
How, the rude one always asking about the strands,
But his control is still in her hands
Who, the churlish one, always disturbs the love angle,
As now no one is there to cherish the sweet little angel
When, the dangerous of all,
Hard to precise
He made her fall,
He let her rise
Oh, the lonely she,
Waiting for her only he
Looking on those empty streets,
Missing her wishful treats
Her admirer,
Her beauty capturer
Hope her wishes fulfil soon,
Hope she gets the justice soon,
Hope they'll come together soon,
We all can pray
But am pretty sure,
He brought ailment, he'll bring cure
Because,
"Everything is just a moment of time and it pass by."
TIME, her best friend and the worst enemy!!!
Kritzy

4. HALF FULL AND HALF EMPTY

Our survival and wellness require a balance between optimism and pessimism. This poem is focussing on this particular aspect and how optimistic and pessimistic ideologies impacts our nature, our actions and our lives. Have a happy reading!!

One gives hope, another gives sorrow,

Is this the only difference do they borrow?

Is it always about the positiveness with optimist?

Or it is about negative ness with pessimist.

Is it kind of, one brings you success?

And another gives failure that you posses

But after all

Its not about, you win or lose,

Its all about the way you choose

It is about the consciousness of mind,

The solutions of the problem, that you find

It depends upon your way,

On which sometimes you walk and sometimes you lay

Its not only about the dream you chase,

But even the reality that you face

And yes,

One always focuses on the chances,

And another tries to find excuses

It does not depend upon the surroundings where you live in,

But it only depends on you, what you take in

In this one has the outlook to bring light, even in the darkest hour,

Another, even after standing near the goalpost, thinks goal is too far

But above all this, irony we get:

"Optimism let us live our life with a spark,

And pessimism wants us to spend our life in dark."

Kritzy

5. NOT EVERYONE

Some realistic philosophical idea in the box, through which everyone come across at least once in a life. Just dive into it, a little bit!!

Not everyone who is poor, wants to be,

Not everyone who is rich, wants to be

Not everyone who is introvert, wants to be,

Not everyone who is extrovert, wants to be

Not everyone who is smiling, is happy,

Not everyone who is crying, is in grief

Not everyone who fought war, wants it,

Not everyone who wanted war, fights it

Not everyone who speaks truth, is sincere,

Not everyone who is sincere, says it

Not everyone who lies, is deceitful,

Not everyone who is deceitful, actually lie

Not everyone who expresses, is genuine,

Not everyone who hides, is fake

Not everyone who is loving, finds it,

Not everyone who is loathing, lose it

Not everyone who is living, wants to,

Not everyone who is dying, wants to

In fact

Everyone here is struggling with their own vicinities, to

change it
Some in love,
Some in lust
Some in virtues,
Some in sins
Knowingly or unknowingly,
Everyone is playing their part,
To conquer that everyone's heart
In search of diamond, carving their stony fruits,
To make that dreamy castle, digging their firm roots
In all,
Everyone is compromising their actions at the cost of
adjustment,
For the adaptation of inner peace in the world of chaos.
Let them be, just let them be…
Be it right or wrong, its ok
Nature is balancing,
In fact, it is tracing
Everyone's actions and deeds,
After all Karma is supreme, fruits accordingly,
So, trust the process wisely, indeed.
As
"No one who did good, will ever come to bad end…"
Kritzy

6. A LETTER AMIDST THE WORLD OF WHATSAPPS

A letter is a written message conveyed from one person (or group of people) to another through a medium. Historically, letters have existed from ancient India, ancient Egypt and Sumer, through Rome, Greece and China, up to the present day. During the 17th and 18th centuries, letters were used to self-educate. The main purposes of letters were to send information, news and greetings. For some, letters were a way to practice critical reading, self-expressive writing, polemical writing and also exchange ideas with like-minded others. For some people, letters were seen as a written performance. Letters are gradually losing importance in the digital world. This trial is to throw some light on what emotions letters carry with them. We can't ignore their value!!

Dear _____,

How are you?

Hope you are doing great…

Like this I found a letter amidst world of WhatsApp,

And amazed how a piece of paper can make my heart trap

In the web of words strung together,

Made a holy garland of love tied forever

Lemme share a passage verbatim,
From letter itself, with no trim
Where she asked him…
When I first saw you, I felt some unusual,
Did you feel the same?
Like flowers blooming in Vatika,
And breeze cherishing every moment
Did you see those flowers, and felt that breeze the same?
I was able to recognise your nature,
Could you recognise mine?
I saw the struggles in your eyes,
Did you see strives in my vibes?
I saw the strengths, in your arms,
Did you find the same in my calms?
I found your smile enlivening,
Did you find munificence in my giving?
I saw ethics in you firmly rooted,
Did you see morals in me, that's grounded?
I saw your respect, that am ready to respect,
Are you ready to respect, that I too have respect?
I saw the legacy of ethos in you,
Can you take it forward?
I am ready to support you in everywhere, whether it is from
besides or backward
I will always try to justify my name with my actions,
Can you justify the same, with your reactions?
I have seen The Ram in you,

Have you seen The Sita in me?
Waiting for your answers Ram.
Yours Sita
And in this I found, how lord's eternal love looks like,
Maybe, reasonably
I found a letter amidst the world of WhatsApp,
Amazed how a piece of paper can make my heart trap…
Kritzy

7. CARRY ME

Am at my lowest,

Wondering why he closed all the closet

Stuck at a point in life,

Not getting anything to climb

Neither a hand nor a rock,

As stable as on a dock

Its really hard to clean this grime,

Am all alone here, carry me home!!

That home of peace,

Which keeps me in fleece

Where, says every wall,

He may let you fail sometimes, but he will never let you fall…

Please carry me that home!!

Am stuck at a point in life,

Not getting anything to climb…

Kritzy

8. IT HAS TO BE THIS WAY

We rise, we fall,
Then we grow tall
We run, we crawl,
And so, then we are able to roar
We laugh we cry,
In giving and giving a try
We open, we close,
The door, we choose
We break ourselves,
We make ourselves
We isolate, we socialise,
That's how we sell our solidarity on prioritise
We are accepted, we are rejected,
All according to the soul vibes so ejected
We are praised, we are disgraced,
This is how we all get embraced
Either choose to run, or choose to stay,
In the end, it has to be this way
The seas will calm, frequencies will fruits,
And mind will gain its peaceful suits
So,

"Resolutely train yourself to attain peace."
-Gautama Buddha
Kritzy

9. SORROWS OF PARTITION

The first Partition of Bengal (1905) was a territorial reorganization of the Bengal Presidency implemented by the authorities of the British Raj. The reorganization separated the largely Muslim eastern areas from the largely Hindu western areas. Announced on 19 July 1905 by Lord Curzon, the then Viceroy of India, and implemented on 16 October 1905, it was undone a mere six years later. British disregard for public opinion and what they perceived as a "divide and rule" policy. The partition of India in 1947 divided British India into two independent dominions: India and Pakistan. The partition displaced between 10 and 20 million people along religious lines, creating overwhelming calamity in the newly-constituted dominions. It is often described as one of the largest refugee crises in history. There was large-scale violence, with estimates of the loss of life accompanying or preceding the partition disputed and varying between several hundred thousand and two million. The violent nature of the partition created an atmosphere of hostility and suspicion between India and Pakistan that affects their relationship to this day. Sorrows of partition is an experience of the destructive decision through a love story!!

The shh she, the loud he,

The sweet she, the salty he,

The calm she, the warm he,

The shy she, the naughty he,

Have met on the crossroad,

Who knew that would be the moment of betrothed

Of their eyes, in blooming love sighs,

In wintery chilling mornings,

That rosy-posy feelings

Has took their hearts together,

They started falling for each other

But in the mid of their walk,

In the noise of rubbish talk

Their lives took a turn,

Has made them to run

Run from the fight of fear,

That fear of force,

Force that became a cause,

That cause of separation,

Which led by partition,

Has brought their love story to end.

But in their hearts, they stayed forever...

Hoping for the justice,

To all such instincts

That can save togetherness for future,

And let the fondness in minds to nurture

But deep inside, their wounds could never heal,

Those who played in motherland, with full zest and zeal
Have gone somewhere,
One can find it nowhere,
As partition not only divided the land in nations, but also,
The hearts, ideologies, togetherness, enthusiasm and everything
And "Humanity" was above all…
"Partition an apt example of how the particular's plan can ruin the souls of the commons."
Kritzy

10. A HANDFUL OF SOIL

It nurtures the plants,
It nurtures the animals,
It nurtures the insects,
It nurtures the humans,
It nurtures every creature on the earth,
Right starting from their birth, till their death
It nurtures the feelings,
It nurtures the breathings
It quenches the hunger,
It brings everyone out of this danger
It nurtures the bravery,
It nurtures the amory
It nurtures the love,
It nurtures the dove(peace)
It makes everyone,
Everything is made from it
It takes in everything,
Everything gets dissolved in it
In the end,
It is the Soil
Which asks you to give nothing,

But effort, a tiny effort to save it,
From erosion,
Save it from turning to barren sand,
So that it can give you, a decent land
To live with love,
Together with all above
As,
"According to many recent studies only 60 years of harvest soil is left, and can degrade more quickly if not saved. Results will be drastic"
Let's save the soil from dying,
Just grow a plant with our hands on trying…
"Upon this handful of soil, our survival depends. Husband it and it will grow our food, our fuel and our shelter and surrounds us with beauty. Abuse it and the soil will collapse and die, taking humanity with it" -- Proverb Vedic Scripture (1500 BC)
Kritzy

Contact us for book publications

Email: ranjanthapa316@gmail.com